Praise for E

"Breeanna Maree has ⌐
poetry marries truth
type is correct, as one can't say love is an bliss and ... ⌐   ⌐
versa; and the aesthetics/beauty that births ease in the reading,
understanding and enjoying of poetry, as communication isn't
complete, except the recipient of the data understands and possibly
gives feedback."

—Graciano Enwerem (Sir Grrraciano),
author of *Spoken Word Poetry 101*

"The essence of her writing style brings the universe and the earth
together to create an entertaining script of realness for all individuals who enjoy poetry who can relate. *Deception*, *Could It Be?*, and
Welcome Mat were deeply passionate short written poems that
define the struggle of black womanhood, as each poem closes with
a life lesson learned."

—Jamil Smith, spoken word poet and sports ambassador

"[Breeanna] dares to journey into the folds of vulnerability in matters
of emotions in a genderless fashion. These works take you on a journey
and play on your senses. *Bites of Bitter, Sips of Sweet* is must read for all
the romantics and readers seeking to heal and try again."

—Rashid White, author of Love Lust

"...one of the best love-focused poetry novels I have read in a
while. Your ability to intertwine emotion with words, and make
the reader feel a sense of belonging and understanding through
rhyme is extraordinary."

—Tony House, poet

"Breeanna never fails to amaze me and I'm so excited for the individuals who will get to hold her words in this book. There isn't a single poem that isn't breathtaking in some way. Many of them feel like individual performances--as if attending a spoken word in your mind. Others feel like secret love letters. Each poem succeeds, though, in its ability to connect to the reader, whether by connecting them to the pain or the soft beauty of love she conveys."

—Cassidy Bradwell, author of *September Was Yellow Flowers*

"...there is something in this book for everyone, those that are open with their emotions, those who can't find the right words to say and those who are in denial..."

— LeRoi author of *Kola Nut & 'Oney*

"The catharsis of each poem provokes and induces hefty emotions on the readers. The poet made us understand the truth and vicissitudes of human life through metaphors of memories, love, betrayal, grief & regrets."

—Olowo Qudus Opeyemi, author of *Flowers & Thorns*

"The strength of Breeanna's poems I believe, lies in her originality...Her expression, diction and flow was so on point. The use of imagery was epic."

—Gyabaah A. Gerold, also known as performance poet Stranja Depoet

BITES
of BITTER
Sips of Sweet

BREEANNA MAREE

Bites of Bitter, Sips of Sweet
Published by Garden Breeze Media
Lancaster, CA

ISBN: 978-1-7372979-0-1
POETRY / Subjects & Themes / Love & Erotica

Cover and Interior design by Victoria Wolf, wolfdesignandmarketing.com
Illustrations by Ma'Ryiya Davis

Publisher's Cataloging-in-Publication data

Names: Maree, Breeanna, author. | Davis, Ma'Ryiya, illustrator.
Title: Bites of bitter , sips of sweet / written by Breeanna Maree; illustrated by Ma'Ryiya Davis.
Description: Lancaster, CA: Garden Breeze Media, 2022.
Identifiers: ISBN: 978-1-7372979-0-1
Subjects: LCSH Poetry, American. | Love poetry, American. | BISAC POETRY / Subjects & Themes / Love & Erotica
Classification: LCC PS3563.A6444 B58 2022 | DDC 811.54--dc23

QUANTITY PURCHASES: Schools, companies, clubs, and other organizations may qualify for special terms when ordering quantities of this title. For information, email breeannamareecreates@yahoo.com.

Garden Breeze Media

To my family who have taught me the depths of unconditional love. And to those who have stumbled while discovering true love.

Bree Maree

Contents

Sweet

BITTER

BITTER ME SWEET

the cynical side of me
slithers to the surface so frequently i've
lost sight of what hope looks like
standing beside the enemy of hate
i've rushed the gate many times
unsuccessfully
so my heart has grown abundantly fatigued as i
redundantly plea
for mercy
from the torture of a journey to something
beautiful
perhaps life's offering of sweet
cannot be properly savored
without first understanding
the flavor
of bitter

DECEPTION

You trip over doubt
Stumble over disbelief
With eyes fixed on the past
Away from a future you can't see
You
Are led by a heart of fear
Venturing into unsteady waters with ears
Deaf to honesty
And eyes blind to truth
Because love is no tangible investment for you.
Fatigue kicks in
Pulling at your patience with a relentless hand
Until you begin diluting your standards and
Freely embracing delusion.
But this my friend
Is how you fall victim
To love's illusions.

BETRAYAL

What does betrayal look like?
Like *la lengua* pushing through lines of lipstick
That never said I do but know
I don't really have you like
Hands wandering on foreign wonderlands
Unphased by promises on wedding bands like
Unclothed bodies undulating to the beat of breath
Pulsating to every caress of the breast like
The weight of "I love you" in a whisper
Way heavier than the one spoken at the altar like
Beat my heart blue
What does betrayal look like?
It look like bruise.

REVENGE

Two lips curse tulips
to dead blooms
many times before trampled
by big boots
boots that extract empowerment from gloom
and find joy
in defacing forests.
See, your feet found greatness in power found
power in force
burned humility with hubris, a
scornful torch
but that's not what empowered meant
when it clothed your hands in strength
the purpose was not to mold confidence with
destruction.
At most I fear
the power that rests in the atmosphere
of revenge
a taste as sweet as ice cream
but consequences as cold as ice, like
an outstanding balance of retaliation
beneficial only to strife.

You fight, I fight
pushback feels right so
who will end this dance
of monotony?

CODEPENDENCY

my tears trace sorrow
onto cold sheets
growing stiff from the stench
of cold feet
there's no joy found
in lonely
no warmth in this void
that holds me
the shadows whisper your name
the draft carries your touch
in your absence even the sunrise
isn't quite enough
to bring life to soul that's
forgotten how to breathe
this is the bitter hold
of codependency

WELCOME MAT

Here
On this welcome mat
Good men with bad hearts know welcome
Like carpet know stain, they
Take for hostage the souls of good women
Tracking mud onto their floors
And burden onto their hearts
On this welcome mat
Good men with bad mouths mold insecurities into daggers
That dig deep into independent skin of strong women
That know want and need
Are as far from similar
As father and daddy
See, on this welcome mat
Good men with bad habits
Mastered breaking hearts, breaking homes, and breaking promises
Before they learned build her up
So they break her down
Praise her strength then snatch her crown
'Cause there can only be one leader 'round
Here

And that's king
Ain't no room for queens
Well ain't no room for peasants either so pack your things
'Cause here
On *this* welcome mat
Good women with scarred hearts
Teach good men with bad parts
Goodbye.

TONGUE-TIED

in this marriage with unsatisfied
i can't help but wonder if
love is an exclusive pastime
off-limits
to those who can't afford the space or time
to rewind the lies that
encage the mind
a mind preoccupied with
broken ties to "i am"
trying not to drown in "you are"
where does love fit
in a throat that chokes on unworthy
long before "i love you" even reaches the tongue
forgive me for my doubt
but you see
love cannot possibly live here
it would not survive

LOVE AND LOSS

You danced around the house packing your things
I made dinner for two
A familiar dance with denial
But deep down I knew
In some relationships
This relationship
Lows simply accentuate the highs
So why would things be any different *this* time
We are rulers of repetition
Masters of masking recognition
Because problems don't exist if you refuse them
visualization
But when is repetition ever capable of revival?
When this relationship depends upon it for survival
I remember it like it was yesterday
When you abandoned my heart
Vacated our world of all matters of heart
Was this even love?
False euphoria, nothing more
Your heart was never in it
And trust is nevermore
You adopted deceit into your personality
Issues deemed untouchable

Soon became our reality
Lies engulfed our world with flames
Yet I thought
Maybe this can still be saved
If there were something I could do
That would make you stay
I'd do it without question
To give us one more day
Another day of laughter
Shared between two
One more day to hear you say
"I love you"
One more day to caress your face
Between these hands of mine
Another day of tight embrace
Between my longing arms
I'd drop my pride or beg if I had to
I'd do anything if it meant not losing you
Lost
That's what I am without you
I've cried myself an ocean
The deepest shade of blue

There's no limit to my sorrow
No barricade to this grief
Just memories that haunt
And reminders that tease
It feels wicked, this nostalgia
Poison to a longing soul
But I welcome it anyway
Because oh
How I miss you
I sit in the comfort of reminiscence
Cherishing the good times we had
How we engraved our love in time
With the sweet rhythm of dance
But with each step, each slide
Played out in the depths of my memory
I release your laugh, your smile
From the forefront of what's dear to me
Your heart is no longer connected to mine
And I can't help but smile with relief
Because this euphoria will grow with time
And I will finally be
Free.

A HAUNTING

you
like seventy percent cacao on the tongue are
bitter beauty
washed away with every kiss
of new lips
bitter slowly fades back to sweet
until starry skies of the deep
blue night repaint our memories
one thousand strokes a minute
onto this
vulnerable mind running
a thousand miles a minute
when the quiet returns with the light of day
the wave soon follows again
and i am reminded
of what was
and what could have been

BROKEN

A somber heart sings
Melancholy echoes in
Joyless symphony.

STOUT

My heart has grown weary of climb
Too familiar with bruise from hydroplanes yet
When warmth of smile dries the rain
The ascent to love begins again
This itsy bitsy heart of mine
Is more brave than naïve
Chucking up the water spout
Thirsty for misery
It thinks that love waits beyond
A path so slippery
It kicks the wind from my lungs
And leaves me hanging by my teeth
This itsy bitsy heart of mine
So foolish and so stout
Legs heavy with hope
Mind not heavy enough with doubt
Stretches with desperation
For the peak of the climb
Only to realize at the top
There's no love for her to find
Itsy bitsy heart so bruised
You give no time to cower
You don't fear the storm, how could you

You're too accustomed to rain showers
If you hit the ground
You'll look around for every shattered piece
Mold it to the shape of a heart
And make sure that it beats
If a rhythm remains, though it sounds like pain
We'll begin the climb again
And if we fall again
It won't mean the end, just
Repeat
Repeat.

SCARRED

I'm just a hopeless romantic
Whom romance left hopeless.

VACANCY

why does love
abandon my ears
to the sound of dried promises
cracking beneath the weight of tears
that died with the scent of adore
now scattered on my floorboards, i
just want to share
the space in my chest
with requited happiness
instead of stuffing these walls with
vacancy
when will love finally
visit my door

MIDNIGHT BLUES

the midnight chill
traces solitude onto longing shoulders
with ice-cold fingertips
drenching skin
in goosebump constellations
to mirror the night sky
that echoes cries
of abandonment
you left a year ago
but love escaped
much sooner
your presence taught me
how alone can coexist
with two bodies
and your absence taught me
that i in fact
never knew love

GOODBYE

I left yesterday with a kiss,
packed all my things and
wiped my lips
'cause the taste of remember
has grown far too bitter
for today
and tomorrow
promised me sweet.

EUTOPIA

I'm dreaming of a world where
Love isn't futile
A heart on a sleeve is precious
And "I love you" has eternal value.

Sweet

The Wordless Romantic

I'm fist fighting the fear in my heart
to mold affection to words
if they stumble on the way out of my mouth
could you still decipher their worth?
See, love doesn't consume my tongue
the way pessimism does
so if somehow love finds its way to speech, perhaps
you are the one.

Could It Be?

If I told you I loved you
would you believe me
or would you say I lost my mind?
Is love only measured by time or
can it be timed by feeling
I mean what is love, really?
A physical connection, a
mental recollection
of timeless moments?
The definition is unclear
but my soul hears the words so
clearly.
It sounds like having you near, like
"you're beautiful" sitting in the canals of my ear but
I'm not quite sure what that means.
Love isn't something you see with your eyes
but something you see with your heart like
palpitations pressed on my soul as a kiss.
Or goosebumps on my arms
as my name rolls from your throat like thunder
to your lips.
I swear I'm in love but I can't quite work it out
because the only love I've ever seen

is not the kind I want around.
The sort of love that leaves you lifeless and begs you to
drown
I won't lose myself in you though
I just want to share this crown.
Yet I'm doubting this could work, regardless of the perks
seeing the beauty in love is easy but
what about the quirks?
Would you ride the waves with me
keep our boat above the sea
or would you abandon me to shore proving love's capacity
Is confined by walls of self-preservation
suffocated by the smoke of provocation
rising from the flames of distrust, swirling among the
embers of lust?
I shouldn't paint our future
with the color of my past but
the only love I've ever seen didn't last.
So if I told you I loved you
would you say it back?

Euphoria

I tripped and fell
Into love
And out of lonely.

Invasion

i found love at my doorstep
dressed in white chiffon and
rose-colored ribbon
dancing with the wind
i heard it
call to me in a soft whisper a
gentle invitation to
a world masked by fantasy
as if no barrier stood between us
it pulled at my soul
stretching me to depths i
never witnessed before
my body
was consumed by the warmth of its light and
though it had the power to
i was not blinded
instead
i was eaten alive by its magic and
in that moment i knew
love had invaded my heart

Love Sings

Love is like a song
Temporary in the ear
Everlasting on the soul.

Embrace

warm embrace
followed by butterfly frenzy
calls my throat to flames like
sandpaper on windpipe
most would say i'm choked up
i say
once again
love has found beauty
in breathlessness

Soul Mate

is it
too much,
the way i consume you with
soul peering eyes
every inhale a ride on
your spiritual current i
see beyond glass iris
into deep beyond
where secrets untold embrace me
with hungry arms
it's true
i attach myself so
easily to you
lacing myself
in your empty spaces but
when i look in your eyes i
don't just see your eyes i
see your soul
and it's beautiful
so i can't help it
i hope that's not
too much

Rain

like rain on rose petals
your voice tap dances on my soul
vocal symphonies of
"i love you"
drip from your tongue like
sugar water
nourishing this seed
of love

A Taste of Love

A sea of dark chocolate
Something like soul food
But sweeter
Every kiss a taste of cherry atop my
Favorite sundae
You were made
For overindulgence.

Soul Music

you are
rain on a Sunday
a tranquil trance

Sunday Prayer

Sunrays make cocoa-buttered skin glisten
As the summer heat paints melanin in dewdrops.
I drink you up with admiring eyes
In a quiet gaze of gratitude.
My soul pulls at yours
And without a single word off your lips
Yours calls to mine.
Your deep brown cheeks draw up a smile
Before you touch your lips on mine and
I melt into your sweet nostalgia.
You are the taste of
Cinnamon on buttered toast
A warming sip of smooth dark roast
You are summer days in the shade
Iced lemonade in hand
You are the love found in ten fingers intertwined
Two shoulders that carry the weight of my world
So I may carry yours on mine.
You are sweet serenity
Found in quiet days
My world wouldn't be quite the same
Without you.

My blessing to clasped hands
You are
A Sunday prayer.

Selfish

You
are everything dreams are made of
stardust and dusky skies of galaxies you
draw me in with the warmth of a million seas kissed by
the sun
you leave footprints on my memory
when you dance upon my dreams you
superman or superhuman
the way you supersede my expectations of what man can
be
a man that say amen
and in the same breath praises his queen you
spirit of prayer
breath of free I
love you
almost
as much as I love me.

Earl Grey

An aromatic cloud fills my nose
and fogs my senses
as I'm taken from the kitchen table back
to a familiar time,
comfortable like the scent
of Earl Grey tea.
Earl Grey
silky on the tongue
like your name off my lips
a color as deep as its flavor
just like you
melanin rich
as your personality
deep brown and delicious.
The steam fades as I
am brought back to the present
but the memories remain
an imprint on my mind like
a stain
of Earl Grey.

Echo

i whisper your name into the open wind and
listen for its echo
because maybe if the earth remembers your name i
won't be the only one
who can't let go

I Miss You

when i met you i
learned how sanctuary becomes
suffocating how
half-full impersonates half-empty as
i lie alone half-empty in this
half-full bed how
my pillow misses the weight of your head or
maybe that's just my words
impersonating my heart
to try and say
i miss you

Ten Things Love Taught Me

Home is where the heart is
but every heart deserves a home big enough to hold it.
True connection is unspoken.
Love is found in two months,
love is lost in twenty years.
Love isn't perfect
but there are more laughs than tears.
Love is a kiss
but it's also friendship.
My standards aren't too high
just because you don't meet them.
My body is a temple
and you're an atheist.
Lies and sweet nothings
can fall off the same lips.
A durag don't make him a thug
but playing with my heart does.
The only love void of flaws
comes from above.

Acknowledgments

To my family, my gratitude is boundless. You fuel my confidence, replenish my motivation and never doubt my ability. To the rest of my supporters, thank you for believing in me. Your support is invaluable.

Thank you for your support!

About the Author

Breeanna first discovered poetry as a young girl and deepened that connection in adulthood when she began translating her undying need for expression into words on the page. Her passion for the art led her to enter a poetry competition and as a result, in 2018, published a  poem in *Colorism: Essays and Poems Volume 2*. Breeanna's poetry predominantly covers love, the complexities and struggles of blackness, and the struggle and beauty of feminine life. She hopes to give others a voice through her words and to inspire healing through her work. After Breeanna's debut with *Bites of Bitter, Sips of Sweet*, she plans to follow-up with a book of poetry covering the dichotomy in the black experience. To follow more of Breeanna's journey, find her on Instagram as @sincerely_breeanna

Made in the USA
Middletown, DE
05 September 2022

72279986R00046